Will Someone Play Bluey?

by Eileen Ivers

illustrated by Solomiia
at GetYourBookIllustrations

Text and Illustrations copyright © 2021 Eileen Ivers
Published by Musical Bridge Publishing

All rights reserved.
No part of this publication may be reproduced, distributed, or transmitted in any form or by any means, including photocopying, recording, or other electronic or mechanical methods, without the prior written permission of the publisher, except in the case of brief quotations embodied in reviews and certain other noncommercial uses permitted by copyright law.

The moral right of the author and illustrator has been asserted.

Library of Congress Control Number: 2021916254

Publisher's Cataloging-In-Publication Data
(Prepared by The Donohue Group, Inc.)

Names: Ivers, Eileen, author. | Solomiia, illustrator.
Title: Will someone play Bluey? / by Eileen Ivers ; illustrated by Solomiia at GetYourBookIllustrations.
Description: [West Nyack, New York] : Musical Bridge Publishing, [2021] | Interest age level: 004-012. | Summary: "In Eileen's music school, the instruments come to life when the children go home. When Drake the drum and the other instruments bully Bluey the violin for being different, Bluey learns to stand up for himself. It takes a special moment for them to appreciate Bluey and see that his differences are actually his strengths"--Provided by publisher.
Identifiers: ISBN 9781737632108 (hardback) | ISBN 9781737632115 (paperback) | ISBN 9781737632122 (ebook)
Subjects: LCSH: Violin--Juvenile fiction. | Bullying--Juvenile fiction. | Individual differences--Juvenile fiction. | CYAC: Violin--Fiction. | Bullying--Fiction. | Individual differences--Fiction. | LCGFT: Stories in rhyme.
Classification: LCC PZ7.1.I98 Wi 2021 (print) | LCC PZ7.1.I98 (ebook) | DDC [E]--dc23

DEDICATION

For my son, AIDAN,
and for all children
learning the importance
of kindness and respect.

Kids come from around,
    Meet up to make sound,
But ...

"Fee-Fi-Fo-Fooey
No one wants to play Bluey ♪♫♪"

"Fee-Fi-Fo-Fooey!!"

Finn's flute plays so shrill; Joe's banjo frails hard.

Drake gets all the others to let down their guard.

"Stop it! You're hurting Bluey's feelings"

Priscilla stays sweet
And does not repeat
The mean things they say
to *the blue violin.*

The very next day
The children all come,

"That's it!" Bluey shouts, "I've all I can take!"

No kid wants to play me, I've such a HEARTACHE

I'm different, I know, So I'll have to show

Priscilla, his friend,
Is happy to see
Ol' Bluey stand up for
himself and decree,

The children go home,
The school's now all dark,
And Bluey thinks now
is the time to embark.

For he has a switch
That will change his pitch,
Plugs into the amp and emits
such a SPARK!

His color from blue
Turns GOLD
and then RED,

Plays so many songs,
wakes the others
from bed.

He plays slow, then fast,
Oh, what a contrast!

None other can shred
like *the blue violin!*

Priscilla and Finn,
Then Joe
and then Drake,
Jump up from their beds
and are now wide awake.

Much kind words then flowed,

Because Bluey showed
They judged him on looks,
which was such a mistake.

Now Bluey feels great
To make this be known,
That if you are different,
you're not all alone.

Stand up for yourself!
Don't sit on a shelf!
What makes you so special
should proudly be shown.

ABOUT THE AUTHOR

Grammy-awarded recording artist, performer, composer, producer, educator and 9-time All-Ireland Fiddle Champion, Eileen Ivers is known for her unique musical style and her signature blue violin, "Bluey."

Eileen lives in New York with her husband and son. When her son was bullied on the elementary school bus, Eileen was proud to see him learn to return the next day, stand up for himself, ultimately befriending the child. Eileen connects her musical and family experiences in authoring her first children's book.

After graduating *magna cum laude* in mathematics, Eileen Ivers was awarded a Doctor of Arts, *honoris causa*, from her graduate and post graduate alma mater, Iona College, for her "lifelong commitment to innovation, excellence and deep dedication to bringing people together through music."

Eileen and her music can be found online at www.eileenivers.com

Look for the audiobook of *"Will Someone Play Bluey?"* and your child can hear the instruments come to life throughout the book as the author reads in rhyme and rhythm.

CPSIA information can be obtained
at www.ICGtesting.com
Printed in the USA
BVHW090817231121
622340BV00007B/287